Aquarium Fish
QUIZ

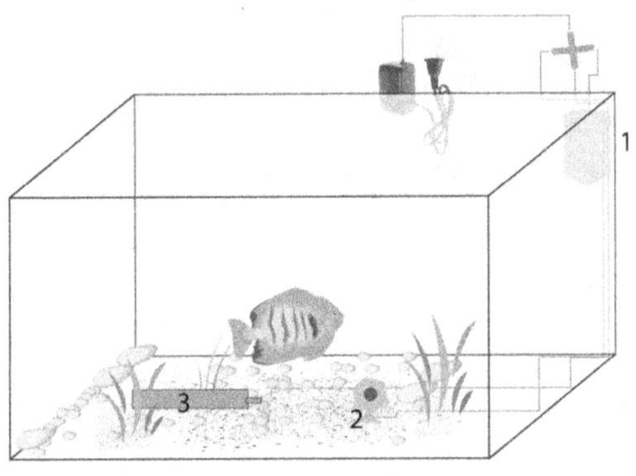

Mundy Obilor Jim

ISBN: 978-82-93422-08-2.

Contents

Prologue

The popularity of a diverse and enormous variety of fish available in fish shops and public aquariums has increased over the last couple of years hence, understanding and learning a bit more about these various types of fish and some of their basic behaviors can offer fish pet lovers some interesting choices.

This book contains a general knowledge, multiple-choice quiz about aquarium and fish-keeping. It is meant to update and fascinate the enthusiastic aquarium devotee.

Most of the questions have been extracted from the book, **Aquarium Making– Fish-keeping & Maintenance** and the answers can be found at the end of the document.

Quiz 1

1. Which of the following is not one of the four types of aquarium systems?

    a.   Freshwater tropical aquarium
    b.   Marine aquarium
    c.   Oceanic aquarium
    d.   Brackish aquarium

2. Which of the statements is not true?

    a.   Float glass is good for aquarium building
    b.   Plexiglass is not easily scratched
    c.   Tempered glass is about four times stronger than ordinary glass
    d.   Both a and c

3. These fish are transparent– you can see right true them

a. Comets
b. Zebra Danio
c. Jewel fish
d. Kribensis

4. This is not a fact about goldfish

a. Goldfish can feed on Pellets, flakes, live food, veggies and fruit
b. The black telescope is not a type of goldfish
c. The Black Moor is one of the slowest swimming goldfish species
d. Goldfish are both fresh water and salt water fish

5. Consider the glass tank in the following figure. What is the approximate capacity of this tank in litres (1 inch = 2.54 cm)? **Hint:** Divide volume in cubic centimeter by 1000 to obtain the volume in litres.

a. 57 litres
b. 20 litres
c. 47 litres
d. 32 litres

6. Using the same figure for the previous question, what is the approximate capacity of this tank in gallons (1 inch = 0.833 feet)? **Hint:** Multiply

volume in cubic feet by 7.47 to obtain the gallon equivalence.

a. 21 gallons
b. 50 gallons
c. 16 gallons
d. 10 gallons

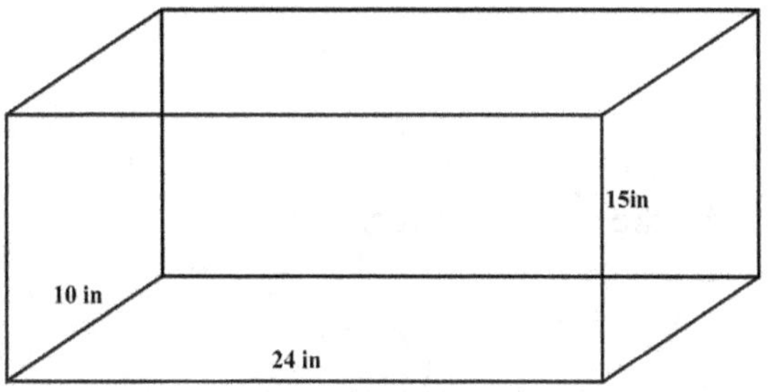

Quiz 2

1. Which of the following is not a system of filtration in the aquarium technology?

   a. Mechanical filters
   b. Nitrogen filters
   c. Chemical filters
   d. Biological filters

2. Only one of these is true

   a. Jewel cichlids (simply called jewel fish) are a native of Asia and are very aggressive in nature
   b. Freshwater angelfish are not aggressive and live together with most aquarium fish
   c. Neon tetras are egg-layers and cannot breed in the fish tank environment
   d. External filters are most suitable when the fish tank is a big size

3. Most people prefer keeping fresh water fish because

    a.   Freshwater fish live longer than saltwater fish
    b.   Freshwater tanks are easy to maintain
    c.   b and c
    d.   It is impossible to maintain saltwater aquarium

4. Which of the following species is a type of the world's most popular aquarium fish?

    a.   Zebra Danio
    b.   Guppies
    c.   Comet
    d.   Black Molly

5. Which is the best relationship between the size of fish and volume of water

    a.   About 100 litres of water per inch of fish
    b.   About 4 litres of water per inch of fish
    c.   25 litres of water per inch of fish
    d.   None of the above

6. Under-gravel filters are

    a.   Not biological filters and they function with special chemicals

b.   Are more effective when the size of grave used is fairly large grains

c.   Biological filters and in some way, act as mechanical filters because they catch solids as they pass into the gravel bed

d.   None of the above

7. PH is the measure of acidity or alkalinity in the water. Which of the following is true?

a.   Most saltwater tanks should have a pH higher than 8.0.

b.   Most freshwater tanks should have a pH of between 6.5 and 7.5.

c.   None of the above

d.   a and b

Quiz 3

1. Cloudy water is USUALLY a sign of

    a. Fungal growth
    b. Disease
    c. Over-feeding
    d. Acidic water

2. When you notice white spots on your fish, it is a sign that there is

    a. Ammonia spike
    b. Ich
    c. No problem
    d. Algae growth

3. Which of the following is not a live-bearer

    a. Guppy

    b. Tilapia
    c. Tetra
    d. Platy

4. Fin rot is usually caused by

    a. Virus
    b. Fungus
    c. a and b
    d. Bacteria infection

5. Glowlight and Sverpae are species of

    a. Goldfish
    b. Tetras
    c. Koi
    d. Guppies

6. Which of the following is not true about angelfish

    a. Angelfish can be nasty and inflict wounds on fish they perceive as a threat
    b. They are easily identified by their angular-shaped body
    c. They are not of the family of cichlids
    d. They are egg-layers

7. Dubai Aquarium has the capacity to hold

   a. About 10million litres of water
   b. Only 2.5 million litres of water
   c. Less than 500 litres of water
   d. None of the above

Quiz 4

1. All of the following can reduce algae growth except

   a. Reduce lighting and exposure to direct sunlight
   b. Change ten to fifteen percent of the aquarium water every week to keep nutrients in the water low
   c. Increase the amount of fish food
   d. Keep live plants as they will use a lot of the nutrients that algae depend upon.

2. The most common tropical fish disease in the aquarium setting is

   a. Fin rot
   b. Ich
   c. Fluke
   d. Fungal infection

3. Which of these fish diseases is parasitic in nature?

    a.   All fish diseases are bacteria related
    b.   Ich
    c.   Fin rot
    d.   None of the above

4. The following increase outbreaks of fungal infections

    a.   Poor water quality
    b.   Injured fish
    c.   Dead fish or large amounts of decomposing organic material in the aquarium
    d.   None of the above

5. What does '*New tank syndrome*' mean?

    a.   Excess chlorine in the aquarium
    b.   The urge to purchase a new fish tank
    c.   The fish are living with a high level of ammonia
    d.   Overfeeding of fish

6. This is not a fact about dropsy

    a.   It is only associated with goldfish
    b.   It is usually fatal to fish

c. It is often characterized by swelling of the fish's abdomen
d. The fish will usually lose appetite

Quiz 5

1. This is of the species of goldfish

    a. Long Nose
    b. Bubble Eye
    c. Alestes
    d. Gouramis

2. This fish has a single tail with nacreous scales
   and a pattern known as calico.

    a. Veiltail
    b. Oranda
    c. Fantail
    d. Shubunkin

3. The scientific name for goldfish

    a. Danio Lineatus
    b. Cyprinus Rerio
    c. Carassius Auratus
    d. None of the above

4. Goldfish can live in harmony with angelfish

    a. Always True
    b. Both are freshwater fish with different needs and should not be housed together
    c. Goldfish are cichlids and will attack angelfish
    d. Angelfish are not egg-layers and should be kept alone

5. Goldfish do live and sleep with their eyes open. They are omnivorous.

    a. False
    b. True
    c. They are saltwater fish
    d. b and c

6. Which of the following is false

    a. Goldfish do not have stomach like other animals
    b. The food they eat passes through the intestines and is immediately excreted

c. Overfeeding goldfish results in overeating which can contaminate the water

d. Goldfish do not produce too much waste and that is why a filter is not needed to keep the water clean

Quiz 6

1. This can possibly fix cloudy aquarium water

    a.   Carry out a 25% change of the existing water
    b.   An upgrade to a more efficient or better filter or adding a second filter
    c.   Doubling the number of fish
    d.   a and b

2. Ammonia is created by waste such as extra food and fish waste. The nitrogen cycle is in this order

    a.   Ammonia > Nitrate > Nitrite
    b.   Ammonia > Nitrite > Nitrate
    c.   Nitrite > Nitrate > Ammonia
    d.   Nitrate > Nitrite > Ammonia

3. Which of the following should be minimum practice for a water change

    a.   Every four months
    b.   Once in six months
    c.   Weekly
    d.   Monthly

4. Which is true about repairing a leaking aquarium

    a.   Ensure you use 100% nontoxic silicone
    b.   Repair is much more effective when silicone sealant is applied on the inside of the tank
    c.   Inspect the tank for the leaked location before draining out the water
    d.   All of the above
    e.   Only a and c

5. Which of the following is not true about *cycling the tank* before adding fish?

    a.   Bring the water conditions up to where they are healthy for the fish
    b.   It is best to cycle the tank when the fish are already in the aquarium
    c.   The tank can be cycled by adding a little fish food– this will start the cycling process by breaking down the food

6. Which of the following is true?

a. Most cichlids are aggressive and territorial
b. Jewel fish and Cobalt blue are of African origin
c. Tiger barbs are aggressive towards females when mating
d. All of the above

Answers

Life is always about animals.
The rest are extras:
Fungi, protists, moneras.

Quiz 1

---

1. c
2. b
3. b
4. d
5. a
6. c

Quiz 2

1. b
2. d
3. b
4. c
5. b
6. c
7. d

Quiz 3

1. c
2. b
3. c
4. c
5. b
6. c
7. a

Quiz 4

1. *c*
2. b
3. b
4. c
5. c
6. a

Quiz 5

1. b
2. d
3. c
4. b
5. a
6. d

Quiz 6

1. d
2. b
3. d
4. c
5. b
6. d

About The Author

Mundy Obilor Jim has a passion for writing, editing and publishing. His published books are in the Technology, Non-fiction and Poetry genres. Mundy started writing from his time at high school through to University, which saw him as Editor of the faculty & Halls of Residence magazines with a potential audience of over thirty thousand people. His love for writing also transcends into songwriting and music production. Apart from writing, Mundy is a qualified Geophysicist & Project Manager with over 15 years' experience. He also builds and maintains aquariums. Mundy lives in Norway and is married with two children.